50 Noodles Across Nations Recipes

By: Kelly Johnson

Table of Contents

- Pad Thai (Thailand)
- Ramen (Japan)
- Spaghetti Carbonara (Italy)
- Pho (Vietnam)
- Japchae (South Korea)
- Chow Mein (China)
- Mee Goreng (Malaysia)
- Macaroni Pie (Caribbean)
- Laksa (Singapore)
- Lo Mein (China)
- Udon with Tempura (Japan)
- Baked Ziti (Italy/USA)
- Spätzle (Germany)
- Dan Dan Noodles (China)
- Fideuà (Spain)
- Khao Soi (Thailand)
- Lasagna (Italy)

- Pansit Canton (Philippines)
- Ants Climbing a Tree (China)
- Tantanmen (Japan)
- Kuy Teav (Cambodia)
- Lomi (Philippines)
- Soba Salad (Japan)
- Goulash Noodles (Hungary)
- Stir-Fried Glass Noodles (Thailand)
- Cold Sesame Noodles (China)
- Tagliatelle al Ragù (Italy)
- Saimin (Hawaii)
- Noodle Kugel (Jewish)
- Fettuccine Alfredo (Italy/USA)
- Yakisoba (Japan)
- Butter Chicken Pasta (India Fusion)
- Hokkien Mee (Singapore/Malaysia)
- Bun Thit Nuong (Vietnam)
- Chicken Stroganoff with Noodles (Russia/Brazil)
- Pasta Puttanesca (Italy)

- Glass Noodle Soup (Thailand)
- Tunisian Couscous with Vermicelli
- Chicken Paprikash with Noodles (Hungary)
- Tsukemen (Japan)
- Stir-Fried Rice Noodles (Vietnam)
- Cacio e Pepe (Italy)
- Vermicelli Upma (India)
- Soba in Dashi Broth (Japan)
- Shanghai Fried Noodles (China)
- Bún Riêu (Vietnam)
- Egg Curry with Noodles (India Fusion)
- Stir-Fried Ramen (Fusion)
- Noodle Salad with Peanut Sauce (Southeast Asia)
- Crab Pasta with Chili (Italy/Singapore fusion)

Pad Thai (Thailand)

Ingredients:

- Rice noodles (soaked)
- Shrimp or chicken
- 2 eggs
- Garlic, chopped
- Bean sprouts, green onions
- Crushed peanuts & lime wedges

Sauce:

- 3 tbsp tamarind paste
- 2 tbsp fish sauce
- 1 tbsp sugar
- 1 tsp chili flakes

Instructions:

1. Stir-fry garlic and protein. Add eggs, scramble.
2. Add noodles and sauce, toss well.
3. Add bean sprouts, green onions.
4. Serve with lime and peanuts.

Ramen (Japan)

Base options: Shoyu (soy), Miso, Tonkotsu (pork bone)
Toppings:

- Soft-boiled egg
- Chashu pork
- Bamboo shoots
- Green onions
- Nori

Instructions:

1. Simmer broth of choice with aromatics.
2. Boil ramen noodles separately.
3. Add noodles to bowl, pour over hot broth.
4. Top with garnishes and enjoy hot.

Spaghetti Carbonara (Italy)

Ingredients:

- Spaghetti
- 2 eggs + 1 yolk
- 1/2 cup grated Pecorino Romano
- Guanciale or pancetta
- Freshly cracked pepper

Instructions:

1. Fry guanciale until crisp. Cook pasta al dente.
2. Mix eggs, cheese, and pepper in a bowl.
3. Toss hot pasta with guanciale, then egg mixture off heat.
4. Stir until creamy. Serve immediately.

Pho (Vietnam)

Broth:

- Beef bones simmered with star anise, cloves, cinnamon, ginger, onion

Noodles & Garnishes:

- Flat rice noodles
- Sliced raw beef
- Bean sprouts, Thai basil, lime, chili

Instructions:

1. Simmer broth for 6+ hours for rich flavor.
2. Boil noodles separately.
3. Add noodles and raw beef to bowl, pour hot broth over.
4. Garnish generously.

Japchae (South Korea)

Ingredients:

- Sweet potato glass noodles
- Beef slices
- Spinach, carrots, onions, mushrooms
- Soy sauce, sesame oil, sugar

Instructions:

1. Cook noodles and rinse in cold water.
2. Stir-fry vegetables and beef separately.
3. Mix all with soy sauce, sesame oil, and sugar.
4. Serve warm or chilled with sesame seeds.

Chow Mein (China)

Ingredients:

- Egg noodles
- Chicken, beef, or shrimp
- Cabbage, carrots, bell peppers
- Soy sauce, oyster sauce, sesame oil

Instructions:

1. Parboil noodles and set aside.
2. Stir-fry meat, then veggies.
3. Add noodles and sauces, stir-fry until caramelized.
4. Serve hot.

Mee Goreng (Malaysia)

Ingredients:

- Yellow egg noodles
- Shrimp or tofu
- Garlic, shallots, chilies
- Tomato ketchup, soy sauce, sambal, lime
- Cabbage, bean sprouts

Instructions:

1. Stir-fry aromatics, add shrimp/tofu.
2. Add noodles, veggies, and sauce mix.
3. Toss on high heat until everything's coated.
4. Serve with lime and crispy shallots.

Macaroni Pie (Caribbean)

Ingredients:

- Elbow macaroni
- Cheddar cheese
- Milk, egg
- Mustard, paprika, black pepper

Instructions:

1. Boil macaroni, mix with cheese, milk, and beaten egg.
2. Add seasonings and pour into a greased dish.
3. Top with extra cheese. Bake at 375°F for 30 mins.
4. Slice and serve warm.

Laksa (Singapore/Malaysia)

Ingredients:

- Rice noodles
- Shrimp or chicken
- Laksa paste
- Coconut milk, chicken broth
- Toppings: bean sprouts, boiled egg, tofu puffs, lime

Instructions:

1. Sauté laksa paste, add broth and coconut milk.
2. Simmer protein until cooked.
3. Add cooked noodles to bowl, pour hot soup over.
4. Top with egg, tofu, and lime.

Lo Mein (China)

Ingredients:

- Egg noodles
- Mixed veggies (carrots, bell peppers, cabbage)
- Soy sauce, oyster sauce, sesame oil
- Chicken, beef, or tofu (optional)

Instructions:

1. Boil noodles and drain.
2. Stir-fry protein and veggies.
3. Add noodles and sauce, tossing until glossy.
4. Serve hot with sesame seeds.

Udon with Tempura (Japan)

Ingredients:

- Udon noodles
- Dashi broth (with soy sauce & mirin)
- Shrimp or veggie tempura
- Scallions, nori, and kamaboko (optional)

Instructions:

1. Cook udon noodles.
2. Heat dashi broth.
3. Fry shrimp/veggies in light batter.
4. Serve noodles in broth with tempura on top.

Baked Ziti (Italy/USA)

Ingredients:

- Ziti pasta
- Ricotta, mozzarella, parmesan
- Marinara or meat sauce
- Italian herbs

Instructions:

1. Cook ziti and mix with sauce and cheeses.
2. Layer in baking dish, top with more cheese.
3. Bake at 375°F for 25–30 minutes.
4. Serve hot and melty.

Spätzle (Germany)

Ingredients:

- Eggs, flour, milk
- Butter
- Nutmeg, salt

Instructions:

1. Mix dough and press through a spätzle maker into boiling water.
2. When they float, sauté in butter until golden.
3. Serve with gravy or cheese.

Dan Dan Noodles (China)

Ingredients:

- Wheat noodles
- Ground pork
- Chili oil, soy sauce, black vinegar, Sichuan peppercorns
- Pickled mustard greens (ya cai)

Instructions:

1. Cook noodles. Stir-fry pork with ya cai.
2. Mix sauce base in bowl, add noodles and pork.
3. Toss well and top with scallions.

Fideuà (Spain)

Ingredients:

- Short pasta noodles (fideuà)
- Seafood: shrimp, mussels, squid
- Saffron, paprika, tomato, garlic
- Fish stock

Instructions:

1. Toast noodles. Sauté seafood.
2. Add tomato and spices, pour in stock.
3. Simmer uncovered until noodles are tender.
4. Serve with aioli.

Khao Soi (Thailand)

Ingredients:

- Egg noodles (boiled + crispy for topping)
- Coconut milk, red curry paste
- Chicken drumsticks or thighs
- Pickled mustard greens, shallots, lime

Instructions:

1. Simmer chicken in coconut curry broth.
2. Cook noodles separately.
3. Serve with broth, crispy noodles, and garnishes.

Lasagna (Italy)

Ingredients:

- Lasagna noodles
- Meat sauce (beef + tomato)
- Béchamel or ricotta mixture
- Mozzarella & parmesan

Instructions:

1. Layer noodles, sauce, and cheese.
2. Repeat layers and bake at 375°F for 40 mins.
3. Let cool slightly before slicing.

Pansit Canton (Philippines)

Ingredients:

- Egg noodles
- Chicken, shrimp, sausage
- Cabbage, carrots, green beans
- Soy sauce, fish sauce, calamansi juice

Instructions:

1. Sauté protein and veggies.
2. Add noodles and sauce, stir until coated.
3. Serve with calamansi or lime.

Ants Climbing a Tree (China)

Ingredients:

- Glass noodles
- Ground pork
- Garlic, ginger, scallions
- Soy sauce, doubanjiang (chili bean paste)

Instructions:

1. Stir-fry pork with aromatics and chili paste.
2. Add soaked glass noodles and sauce.
3. Toss until noodles soak up the flavor.
4. Serve spicy and savory.

Tantanmen (Japan)

Japanese take on Sichuan Dan Dan noodles

Ingredients:

- Ramen noodles
- Ground pork
- Soy milk or chicken broth, tahini or peanut butter
- Chili oil, garlic, ginger, miso

Instructions:

1. Sauté ground pork with garlic, ginger, miso, and chili oil.
2. Simmer broth with soy milk and tahini.
3. Cook noodles, pour broth over, top with pork.
4. Garnish with scallions and sesame seeds.

Kuy Teav (Cambodia)

Clear rice noodle soup often served for breakfast

Ingredients:

- Rice noodles
- Pork bones or beef stock
- Ground pork, sliced beef, shrimp
- Bean sprouts, fried garlic, scallions, herbs

Instructions:

1. Simmer bones to make a clear broth.
2. Cook noodles and meats.
3. Assemble in bowl with toppings and pour broth over.
4. Add lime juice, chili, or hoisin to taste.

Lomi (Philippines)

Thick egg noodle soup with a hearty, starchy broth

Ingredients:

- Lomi noodles (or thick egg noodles)
- Pork, shrimp, fish balls
- Egg, flour/cornstarch slurry
- Garlic, onion, soy sauce

Instructions:

1. Stir-fry aromatics and proteins.
2. Add water and noodles, simmer.
3. Thicken with starch slurry, stir in beaten egg.
4. Serve hot with calamansi and fried garlic.

Soba Salad (Japan)

Refreshing cold buckwheat noodle dish

Ingredients:

- Soba noodles
- Cucumber, carrot, scallions, edamame
- Soy sauce, sesame oil, rice vinegar, sugar
- Sesame seeds

Instructions:

1. Boil and chill soba.
2. Mix veggies and dressing.
3. Toss together and sprinkle sesame seeds.
4. Serve cold as a light lunch.

Goulash Noodles (Hungary)

A pasta twist on traditional beef goulash

Ingredients:

- Egg noodles or spätzle
- Beef chuck
- Onion, garlic, paprika
- Tomato paste, beef broth, sour cream

Instructions:

1. Brown beef, sauté onions with paprika.
2. Add broth and simmer until tender.
3. Toss sauce with cooked noodles.
4. Serve with a dollop of sour cream.

Stir-Fried Glass Noodles (Thailand)

Savory and slightly sweet dish called Pad Woon Sen

Ingredients:

- Mung bean glass noodles
- Eggs, cabbage, carrots, tofu/shrimp
- Soy sauce, oyster sauce, sugar

Instructions:

1. Soak noodles.
2. Stir-fry vegetables and protein, add eggs.
3. Toss in noodles and sauce.
4. Stir until glossy and cooked through.

Cold Sesame Noodles (China)

Chilled noodles with creamy, nutty sauce

Ingredients:

- Wheat or egg noodles
- Peanut butter or sesame paste
- Soy sauce, vinegar, sugar, garlic
- Cucumber, scallions

Instructions:

1. Cook and chill noodles.
2. Whisk sauce and mix with noodles.
3. Top with julienned cucumber and scallions.
4. Serve cold and refreshing.

Tagliatelle al Ragù (Italy)

Classic Northern Italian pasta dish

Ingredients:

- Tagliatelle pasta
- Ground beef, pork
- Onion, carrot, celery
- Tomato paste, red wine, milk

Instructions:

1. Sauté vegetables, brown meat.
2. Add wine, tomato paste, and milk. Simmer low.
3. Cook pasta and toss with ragù.
4. Top with grated Parmigiano-Reggiano.

Saimin (Hawaii)

Hawaiian noodle soup influenced by Japanese ramen and Chinese mein

Ingredients:

- Wheat noodles
- Dashi or chicken broth
- Kamaboko, char siu, egg, green onion
- Soy sauce

Instructions:

1. Cook noodles.
2. Heat broth with soy sauce.
3. Assemble noodles and toppings in a bowl.
4. Pour hot broth over and serve with chopsticks.

Noodle Kugel (Jewish)

Sweet or savory baked noodle casserole

Ingredients (sweet version):

- Egg noodles
- Eggs, sour cream, cottage cheese
- Sugar, cinnamon, raisins

Instructions:

1. Cook noodles and mix with dairy and eggs.
2. Stir in sugar, cinnamon, and raisins.
3. Bake at 350°F for 45–60 minutes.
4. Serve warm or chilled.

Fettuccine Alfredo (Italy/USA)

Creamy pasta dish originally from Rome, perfected in American kitchens

Ingredients:

- Fettuccine pasta
- Heavy cream, butter, Parmesan
- Salt, pepper, garlic (optional)

Instructions:

1. Cook pasta.
2. Simmer butter and cream, stir in cheese.
3. Toss pasta into sauce, mix until creamy.
4. Top with extra Parmesan and cracked pepper.

Yakisoba (Japan)

Savory stir-fried wheat noodles often served at festivals

Ingredients:

- Yakisoba noodles
- Pork, cabbage, carrots
- Yakisoba sauce (Worcestershire + soy + oyster)
- Pickled ginger, seaweed flakes (optional)

Instructions:

1. Sauté pork and veggies.
2. Add noodles and sauce.
3. Stir-fry until caramelized.
4. Garnish and serve hot.

Butter Chicken Pasta (India Fusion)

Indian-style butter chicken meets creamy pasta comfort

Ingredients:

- Penne or fusilli
- Chicken in butter chicken sauce
- Tomato, cream, garam masala, butter

Instructions:

1. Make butter chicken (or use leftovers).
2. Boil pasta and toss in sauce.
3. Simmer until flavors marry.
4. Serve with cilantro and chili flakes.

Hokkien Mee (Singapore/Malaysia)

Seafood stir-fried noodle dish with rich stock flavor

Ingredients:

- Yellow noodles + rice vermicelli
- Shrimp, squid, egg
- Garlic, sambal, stock, soy sauce

Instructions:

1. Fry garlic and seafood, scramble eggs.
2. Add noodles and rich prawn/chicken stock.
3. Stir-fry with sauces until absorbed.
4. Serve with sambal and lime.

Bun Thit Nuong (Vietnam)

Cold rice noodles with grilled pork and fresh herbs

Ingredients:

- Vermicelli noodles
- Grilled pork, lettuce, herbs, pickled veggies
- Fish sauce dressing (nuoc cham)

Instructions:

1. Marinate and grill pork.
2. Assemble noodles with herbs and vegetables.
3. Top with pork and drizzle nuoc cham.
4. Garnish with peanuts and fried shallots.

Chicken Stroganoff with Noodles (Russia/Brazil)

Comforting dish adapted in Brazil with a creamy tomato twist

Ingredients:

- Egg noodles
- Chicken, onion, garlic
- Tomato paste, cream, mustard

Instructions:

1. Cook chicken with onions and garlic.
2. Stir in tomato paste, mustard, and cream.
3. Simmer and serve over noodles.
4. Sprinkle with parsley.

Pasta Puttanesca (Italy)

Spicy, briny dish rooted in Neapolitan tradition

Ingredients:

- Spaghetti or linguine
- Garlic, anchovies, olives, capers, tomatoes, chili flakes

Instructions:

1. Sauté garlic and anchovies.
2. Add olives, capers, tomatoes.
3. Simmer into a thick sauce.
4. Toss with pasta and finish with parsley.

Glass Noodle Soup (Thailand)

Clear, light broth with mung bean noodles and herbs

Ingredients:

- Glass noodles
- Chicken or shrimp
- Garlic, fish sauce, lime, cilantro

Instructions:

1. Soak noodles and prepare broth.
2. Simmer protein and season.
3. Add noodles last minute.
4. Garnish with herbs and lime.

Tunisian Couscous with Vermicelli

North African dish featuring fluffy grains and spiced stew

Ingredients:

- Couscous and toasted vermicelli
- Lamb or chicken, chickpeas, harissa
- Carrots, zucchini, spices (cumin, coriander)

Instructions:

1. Steam couscous with vermicelli.
2. Cook stew separately.
3. Layer together and serve with harissa.

Chicken Paprikash with Noodles (Hungary)

Hungarian classic with paprika-infused creamy sauce

Ingredients:

- Egg noodles or spaetzle
- Chicken thighs
- Onion, sweet paprika, sour cream

Instructions:

1. Sauté onions, then brown chicken.
2. Add paprika and simmer with broth.
3. Finish with sour cream.
4. Serve over buttery noodles.

Tsukemen (Japan)

Cold dipping ramen with intense, flavorful broth

Ingredients:

- Thick ramen noodles (served cold)
- Dipping broth: pork or chicken base, soy, dashi, bonito, vinegar
- Toppings: chashu, egg, nori, scallions

Instructions:

1. Simmer broth until rich and reduced.
2. Cook and chill noodles separately.
3. Serve with toppings and dip noodles bite by bite.

Stir-Fried Rice Noodles (Vietnam)

Quick wok-fried noodles loaded with veggies and protein

Ingredients:

- Rice noodles
- Shrimp, chicken, or tofu
- Bean sprouts, onion, garlic, fish sauce, soy

Instructions:

1. Soak noodles until pliable.
2. Stir-fry garlic and protein.
3. Add noodles, seasonings, and veggies.
4. Finish with lime and herbs.

Cacio e Pepe (Italy)

Pasta in its most minimalist, magical form

Ingredients:

- Spaghetti or tonnarelli
- Pecorino Romano
- Cracked black pepper

Instructions:

1. Cook pasta and reserve water.
2. Toast pepper in a pan, add pasta water.
3. Stir in cheese and pasta, creating a creamy emulsion.
4. Serve immediately.

Vermicelli Upma (India)

South Indian breakfast dish with savory spiced noodles

Ingredients:

- Roasted vermicelli
- Mustard seeds, curry leaves, chilies
- Onion, peas, carrots, turmeric

Instructions:

1. Fry spices in oil, sauté veggies.
2. Add vermicelli and water.
3. Cook covered until fluffy and absorbed.
4. Garnish with cilantro and lemon.

Soba in Dashi Broth (Japan)

Nutty buckwheat noodles in a light, umami broth
Ingredients:

- Soba noodles
- Dashi stock, soy sauce, mirin
- Scallions, mushrooms, nori

Instructions:

1. Make dashi broth and season.
2. Boil soba, rinse under cold water.
3. Reheat in broth or serve cold separately.
4. Add toppings and enjoy.

Shanghai Fried Noodles (China)

Thick, chewy noodles stir-fried in sweet soy sauce

Ingredients:

- Shanghai-style thick noodles
- Pork, bok choy, mushrooms
- Dark soy, light soy, sugar, garlic

Instructions:

1. Sauté pork and veggies.
2. Add cooked noodles and sauces.
3. Stir-fry until glossy and caramelized.
4. Serve piping hot.

Bún Riêu (Vietnam)

Tomato-based crab and rice noodle soup with bold tang and richness

Ingredients:

- Rice vermicelli
- Crab paste (with egg), tomatoes
- Shrimp paste, tofu, scallions, lime, herbs

Instructions:

1. Make a broth with tomatoes, shrimp paste, and aromatics.
2. Add crab mixture and tofu.
3. Serve with noodles and fresh herbs (mint, perilla, bean sprouts).
4. Finish with lime and chili.

Egg Curry with Noodles (India Fusion)

A comforting, spicy curry poured over noodles instead of rice

Ingredients:

- Boiled eggs
- Curry base: onion, garlic, tomato, garam masala, turmeric
- Noodles of choice (egg noodles or spaghetti)

Instructions:

1. Prepare the curry sauce until thick and aromatic.
2. Add boiled eggs and simmer.
3. Serve over warm noodles or stir-fry together.
4. Garnish with coriander.

Stir-Fried Ramen (Fusion)

Quick comfort dish using instant noodles with a punch

Ingredients:

- Instant ramen noodles
- Soy sauce, sesame oil, garlic, sriracha
- Optional: egg, veggies, leftover meat

Instructions:

1. Boil ramen, then drain.
2. Sauté garlic, then veggies/protein.
3. Toss in noodles and sauce.
4. Top with a fried egg or scallions.

Noodle Salad with Peanut Sauce (Southeast Asia)

Cold, crunchy, creamy, and spicy — perfect for hot days

Ingredients:

- Rice noodles or vermicelli
- Shredded carrots, cabbage, herbs, cucumber
- Peanut sauce: peanut butter, lime, soy, garlic, chili

Instructions:

1. Cook and cool noodles.
2. Whisk up sauce.
3. Toss veggies and noodles in dressing.
4. Garnish with crushed peanuts and cilantro.

Crab Pasta with Chili (Italy/Singapore Fusion)

A luxurious, spicy seafood pasta dish with global roots

Ingredients:

- Spaghetti or linguine
- Crab meat
- Garlic, chili flakes, lemon zest, white wine
- Olive oil, parsley

Instructions:

1. Sauté garlic and chili in olive oil.
2. Add crab and a splash of wine.
3. Toss in pasta and coat evenly.
4. Finish with lemon zest and fresh herbs.

www.ingramcontent.com/pod-product-compliance
Lightning Source LLC
LaVergne TN
LVHW081327060526
838201LV00055B/2494